Interesting

Football

Trivia Book

BY

CHUKU MICHAEL

Note from the Author

As this book ages, answers to some questions that are date-related and that are correct as of September 2022, may likely change. However such questions are relatively small in number.

Disclaimer

I have done all the hard work to make sure that every answer contained in this book is correct and accurate. I however cannot accept responsibility for losses resulting from mistakes, errors, or omissions in this book. Please contact info@funsided.com if you discover an error or omission in this book.

TABLE OF CONTENTS

American Football Trivia Questions

1. Which city hosted Super Bowl I?

2. The Super Bowl XXXVII was hosted in which city?

3. How many Super Bowl championships have the Buccaneers won as of 2021?

4. For a kicked conversion of a touchdown, how many points does the player get in the NFL?

5. Which Stadium does Miami Dolphins play its home games?

6. What is the name of the NFL referee known for wearing tight shirts and flexing for the camera?

7. Which Super Bowl did Michael Jackson perform in?

8. Which year did the Dallas Texans move to Kansas City?

9. How many yards long is a standard NFL football field?

10. Which year was David Tyree drafted by the New York Giants?

11. Which year did the Minnesota Vikings team make their debut in the NFL?

12. Which NFL team drafted Zach Thomas into NFL?

13. Who was the Miami Dolphins' first head coach?

14. Bengals are based in which city?

15. Which year did Sunday night football (SNF) start airing on NBC?

16. What position did Daniel Jones play in New York Giants?

17. The NFL team from San Francisco is called?

18. Atlanta Falcons is a member club of the league's National Football Conference (NFC) in which division?

19. Josh Freeman was released halfway through the 2013 NFL season by which team?

20. The NFC East division has how many member clubs in 2021?

21. Which quarterback threw for the most yards in the 2021 NFL season?

22. The NFL team from Arizona is?

23. Where is Paul Brown Stadium located?

24. The NFL team from Indianapolis is called?

25. Which person won the 2012 NFL MVP award?

26. The NFL team that was the center of a bullying scandal in 2013 was?

27. Jacksonville hosted the Super Bowl how many times as of 2015?

28. Raiders are based in which city?

29. Which Stadium hosted the super bowl XLV?

30. Where did Zach Thomas play college football?

31. The nickname of a San Diego-based NFL team is?

32. The famous helmet catch in the super bowl was made by which wide receiver?

33. How many stars are in the NFL logo?

34. Which NFL team is based in Kansas City?

35. Who has the most passing touchdowns in NFL history?

36. What position did Vince Young play in the NFL?

37. How many cities in Minnesota have hosted the NFL super bowl?

38. The NFL team, Bears, are based in which city?

39. The NFL team from Cleveland is known as?

40. How many seasons did Calvin Johnson play in the NFL?

41. What is Derrick Thomas's nickname in the NFL?

42. The NFL team from Charlotte is called?

43. Which player was drafted first in the 1999 NFL draft?

44. The first loser in Super Bowl III in 1996 was?

45. The NFL team from Dallas is known as?

46. Which year did the 49ers win the first NFL championship

47. The team in the NFL, based in Philadelphia is called?

48. The losers of the Super Bowl XLIII in 2009 were?

49. Super Bowl XVIII was held in which city?

50. San Diego first hosted the Super Bowl in which year?

51. What is the name of the first overall player picked by the St Louis Rams in the 2010 NFL draft?

52. What is the name of the first player that rushed for a record of 2105 yards in the 1984 NFL season?

53. Super Bowl VI was held in which Stadium?

54. Which year did Greg Jennings join the Minnesota Vikings from the Green Bay Packers?

55. During Super Bowl XXXVIII, which player kicked the game-winning field goal?

56. What stadium do the Dallas Cowboys play their home games in?

57. Which Stadium was the Super Bowl XXXVIII held?

58. Which position did the NFL player Keyshawn Johnson play in?

59. How many seasons did Alex Smith play in NFL?

60. Which NFL team did Greg Jennings first play in?

61. How many yards was the famous super bowl field goal known as "wide right"?

62. In which year did Alex Smith join the Kansas City Chiefs from the 49ers?

63. How wide is an NFL football field?

64. The super bowl XXVII was hosted by which city?

65. The New York Giants play their home game in which stadium?

66. The NFL team that has won the most super bowls in 2022 is?

67. The city that hosted Super Bowl IX was?

68. Which position does Eddie Kennison play in?

69. What is the name of the players whose showboating cost him a touchdown at the super bowl XXVII?

70. Which person is credited for coining the name, Super Bowl?

71. The nickname of the NFL star Ben Jarvus Green Ellis is?

72. Jim Thorpe is a Native American, true or false?

73. The NFL team that played only a year in Philadelphia in 1930 was?

74. What is Brett Favre's nickname?

75. What is Brett Favre's position?

76. The Lions are based in which city?

77. The first three Super Bowls the New England Patriots played in were in which city?

78. During the 2013 season, which NFL coach went on medical leave?

79. During Super Bowl XXXVII, which player kicked the game-winning field goal?

80. Which position did Marvin Harrison play in?

81. Where was the super bowl XXVIII held?

82. In which year was Keyshawn Johnson drafted into the NFL?

83. Which position does Terry Glenn play?

84. Jake Long joined the 49ers from Dolphins in 2013, true or false?

85. The 2013 NFL draft took place in which city?

86. In 2013, Jake Long joined which team?

87. In 2013, who replaced Ken Whisenhunt as head coach of the Arizona Cardinals?

88. Thurman Thomas' rush for the Super Bowl XXVII was how many yards?

89. Texans are based in which city in the NFL?

90. The Jaguars are located in which city?

91. The player that joked the Seattle Seahawks from the Detroit Lions in 2013 was?

92. What was the prominent position of Walter Payton?

93. Dallas first hosted the super bowl in which year?

94. What is the name of Julius Jones' brother?

95. What is the position of Julius Jones' brother?

96. Which person won the football coach of the year in 2010?

97. Don Shula won his first coach of the year awards in which year?

98. Larry Alien was inducted into the NFL hall of fame in which year?

99. What is the name of the first president of the NFL?

100. In 2013, what was the number of NFL coach of the year awards Bill Belichick had?

101. How many times has Miami hosted the Super Bowl as of 2020?

102. The city that hosted the super bowl XV was?

103. Which head coach of the Texans was fired in 2013?

104. Super Bowl VII was hosted by?

105. The super bowl XXXVI was hosted in which city?

106. What is the nickname of the NFL team based in Arizona?

107. Super Bowl XLVI was hosted in which city?

108. The nickname of the NFL team based in New Orleans is called?

109. Which position does Tom Brady play?

110. How many catches did Anquan Bordin make during his rookie season at Arizona Cardinals?

111. The PFWA NFL executive of the year in 2013 was won by who?

112. Which year was Muhsin Muhammad drafted as a wide receiver into NFL?

113. Which city hosted Super Bowl XIV?

114. The super bowl XLVIII was held in which city?

115. When did the Super Bowl Era begin?

116. Which team won the most championships before the Super Bowl Era?

117. The New York Giants once won the super bowl and didn't make the playoffs the next season. True or false?

118. In 1987, the New York Giants won the super bowl against which team?

119. The New York Giants won Super Bowl against which team in 1991?

120. Derrick Mayes was drafted as a wide receiver in 1996, true or false?

121. Eric Moulds was drafted as a quarterback in 1996, true or false?

122. That first championship the Green Bay Packers won was in which year?

123. The Green Bay Packers won their thirteenth championship in which year?

124. In 1966, the New York Giants lost 72-41 to which team?

125. The game between Georgia Tech and Cumberland College on Oct 7, 1916, ended in which combined score?

126. The first team to score more than 560 points in a season was?

127. The team that set the record of playing 24 consecutive games and winning all is?

128. The team that set the record of playing 26 consecutive games and losing all is?

129. The Canton franchise began in which year?

130. When did the New England Patriots score 589 points in a season, setting a record?

131. The Canton franchise folded in which year?

132. The first coach to win three NFL coach of the year awards was?

133. The first person that won the coach of the year award was?

134. Bill Cowher was the head coach of a team for more than 10 years, true or false?

135. How many years did Bill Cowher stay at Pittsburgh Steelers as a coach?

136. How many seasons did Don Shula stay at Miami Dolphins?

137. The first African-American quarterback to pass 3000 yards in a season was?

138. The NFL Rams franchise has played in Los Angeles, true or false?

139. Which team did Doug Williams play during his rookie season?

140. The fourth stadium used by the Ram franchise was?

141. AL Davis was born in which place?

142. When was Milner elected into the hall of fame?

143. When was Long elected into the hall of fame?

144. The first lead coach of the Green Bay Packers was?

145. The second lead coach of the Green Bay Packers was?

146. Which club did Morten Anderson retire in in 2004?

147. Earl Curley started coaching Green Bay Packers in which year?

148. Which position does Steve Van Buren play?

149. Which team did Steve Van Buren play for in 1945?

150. During his professional career, which position did Dick Butkus play?

151. During his professional career, which position did George Halas play?

152. How many wide receivers were selected in the 1996 NFL draft?

153. The runner-up of the 2004 rushing title was?

154. Which person won the rushing title in 2004?

155. Deion Sanders came out of retirement in 2004 to play for which team?

156. How many super bowls did Deion Sanders win with the Dallas Cowboys?

157. In 1943, the Chicago Bears lost the NFL championship to which team?

158. Has Morten Anderson played for the Giants in the past? Yes or No?

159. Marty Mornhinweg was once the head coach of the Detroit Lions, True or False?

160. The kicker that threw an interception in Super Bowl VII was?

161. Which team in 1972 finished the season undefeated?

162. When Dan Reeves was the head coach of the Atlanta Falcons, did he lose Super Bowl XXXIII? Yes or No?

163. The team that drafted and cut Bill Parcells in 1964 was?

164. Mark Brunell and Jeff George tied as The AFC's top-rated passers, True or False?

165. What was Morten Anderson's position for the Falcons?

166. In the seventh round of the 1982 NFL draft, which team drafted Gary Anderson?

167. After being drafted by the Buffalo Bills, did Gary Anderson later play for them? Yes or No?

168. Everson Walls was once a member of the Dallas Cowboys, True or False?

169. When did Herchel Walker join the New Jersey Generals?

170. Billy Sims went to college where?

171. Wilbert Montgomery ended his career with the Philadelphia Eagles with how many career yards?

172. What is the name of the team that drafted Johnny Unitas?

173. In super bowl VI, the Miami Dolphins lost to which team?

174. How many yards did Michael Westbrook score in their first NFL game?

175. Michael Strahan ended his career with how many sacks?

176. Kevin Greene ended his career with how many sacks?

177. The first AFL season was in which year?

178. Reggie White ended his career with how many sacks?

179. Bruce Smith ended his career with how many sacks?

180. How many seasons did Eric Dickerson play with the Rams before leaving in 1987?

181. How many games did Eric Dickerson play for Indianapolis Colts in 1987?

182. In the 2010 season, who was the oldest player that played?

183. In his career how many coaching jobs did John Heisman have?

184. John Carney was born in which year?

185. John Carney's 23rd season in the NFL was in which year?

186. How many points did Houston Oilers score in 1961?

187. Which team won the first AFL crown?

188. What was Morten Anderson's position for the Saints?

189. The fourth Pittsburgh Steeler to win the super bowl MVP is?

190. The third stadium sued by the NFL Oakland is?

191. David Givens once played for the New England Patriots, true or false?

192. The New England Patriots won their second NFL championship in which super bowl?

193. Which position does Johnny Lujack play in?

194. The larger seating capacity in the NFL in 2006 was?

195. How many times has Lou Groza been named an All-NFL tackle?

196. Who was the NFL player of the year in 1954?

197. Brett Favre began his career with?

198. What seating capacity did the FedEx field have in 2006?

199. After his first season, Brett Favre went to Green Bay and played how many games?

200. How many mumbles did Warren Moon recover in his career?

201. In the 2003 season, how many teams were in the NFL?

202. Did Washington Redskins play in the 2003 NFL? yes or no?

203. Rich Karlis missed a 23-yard field goal in super bowl XXI, true or false?

204. The NFL MVP award was won by who in the 1985 season?

205. Which position did Marcus Allen play in 1985?

206. Iheanyi Unwazuroke has played for the San Francisco 49ers in the past. True or false?

207. How many TDs did Billy Sims score for the Detroit Lions in his first season?

208. Which potion does Billy Sims play?

209. The first running back in NFL history to record 1000 yards rushing and receiving in one season is?

210. The team that won the inaugural world bowl was?

211. Which team did Roger Craig play for in 1995?

212. The world bowl died many years after being established and was reborn as what?

213. The first player on the losing team to receive a super bowl MVP is?

214. Don Hutson has led the NFL scoring five times in his career, true or false?

215. Which team drafted Brett Favre?

216. Brett Favre played as a fourth-string quarterback for the Falcons, true or false?

217. Norm Van Brocklin never passed for 554 yards as a quarterback, true or false?

218. 1n 2004, John Lynch signed for which team?

219. John Lynch is known as one of the hardest-hitting _____ in the NFL.

220. Bill Goldberg was once drafted into the NFL, True or False?

221. The Rams began to play in which city?

222. Jerry Rice's record of consecutive games with an NFL reception ended in which year?

223. Who was behind Jerry Rice in 2004 in terms of consecutive games?

224. The only team in 2003 to have one primary color on their helmets with no symbols or images was?

225. Michael Strahan set the record for 225 sacks in a season in which year?

226. Jason Elam once played for the Denver Broncos, true or false?

227. Which team was Tom Dempsey in when he kicked his 63-yard field goal in 1970?

228. Tom Dempsey was born without what?

229. Between 1920 to 2000, the Cardinals made how many playoff appearances?

230. The Cardinals started playing in the NFL in which year?

231. Who took over as coach of the Tampa Bay Buccaneers in 1976?

232. When did John McKay die?

233. In which year's NFL draft was Dan Marino picked?

234. Who was picked first overall in the 1985 NFL draft?

235. After the Tampa Bay Buccaneers were introduced in the NFL, they were placed in which division?

236. The Tampa Bay Buccaneers have been in the NFC Central division, true or false?

237. Barry Sanders scored 15 touchdowns in 1997, true or false?

238. Davis of the Broncos had 15 touchdowns in the NFL 1997 season, true or false?

239. When did Johnny Unitas pass 30 touchdowns in one single season?

240. How many 100-yard backs did Cleveland Browns produce in 1985?

241. The team that won the first and inky XFL championship was?

242. How many career receptions does Walter Payton have for the Chicago Bears?

243. Eric Dickerson ran how many yards against the Cowboys?

244. Rashaan Salaam once rushed 1074 yards, true or false?

245. The team that won the NFL championship in 1920 was?

246. The Akron Pros existed until which year?

247. When did Rashaan Salaam rush for 1074 yards?

248. The first NFL team to win 700 games is?

249. Chicago Bears surpassed the 600 wins made in which year?

250. When did the Chicago Bears have their first 700 wins?

251. The Arizona Cardinals joined the NFL in which year?

252. Arizona Cardinals moved to St Louis in which year?

253. The University that won the first BCS championship was?

254. Which position did Tee Martins play for the University of Tennessee?

255. The first team to beat their opponents by 25 points in a game was?

256. Lou Groza Cleveland's career lasted for how many years?

257. In 2004, Jerry Rice ended with how many consecutive games?

258. Sammy Baugh once threw 4 touchdowns and intercepted the ball 4 times in one game. True or false?

259. The Boston bulldogs were originally known as?

260. Which team did Norm Van Brocklin pass 554 yards for?

261. In which year did Sammy Baugh propel the Washington Redskins into a 42-20 victory against the Detroit lions?

262. How many interceptions did Sammy Baugh have in 1943?

263. The first player to win five super bowl rings was?

264. Charles Haley won the super bowl XXIII with?

265. When did Charles Haley retire?

266. The first team to average 30 points per game and have a losing record is?

267. How many points did the Kansas City Chiefs score in 2004?

268. How many points did the Kansas City Chiefs give up in 2004?

269. Johnny Unitas is in the hall of fame, true or false?

270. Where did Johnny Unitas retire?

271. Johnny Unitas's final season was in which year?

272. After retiring, how many years did it take Johnny Unitas to be inducted into the hall of fame?

273. Who won the first NFL defensive player of the year?

274. When did the NFL start giving out the defensive player of the year award?

275. The second defensive player of the year award Joe Greene won was in which year?

276. The first head coach to make four super bowl appearances was?

277. Who was the head coach of the Baltimore Colts in Super Bowl III?

278. Robert Hubbard was inducted into the hall of fame in which year?

279. Robert Hubbard was inducted into the hall of fame one year after his death, true or false?

280. The fourth overall player selected in the 2003 draft was?

281. At the University of Kentucky, which position did Dewayne Robertson play?

282. The third team to defeat the Philadelphia Eagles in the 2003 NFL championship game was?

283. The second-round draft pick of the Carolina Panthers in 1996 was?

284. The first championship Cleveland Browns won was against which team?

285. In which year did the Cleveland Browns join the NFL?

286. The Cleveland Browns won their first NFL championship in their inaugural year, true or false?

287. Which position did John Huarte play?

288. John Huarte played for the Philadelphia Eagles in which year?

289. John Huarte played for the Chicago Bears in which year?

290. Robert Hubbard was inducted into the hall of fame one year before his death. True or False?

291. Reggie Bush is not a native Californian, true or false?

292. The first quarterback that attempted 9000 passes was?

293. How many seasons did Brett Favre play with the Packers?

294. Which position did Bob Scarpitto play in?

295. Brooklyn Dodgers changed their name to?

296. How many seasons did the Brooklyn Dodgers play in the NFL?

297. The fourth head coach of the NFL New York Giants was?

298. When did Folwell coach the New York Giants?

299. The third head coach of the 49ers was?

300. The second home/stadium of the NFL New York Giants was?

301. The APFA later became the NFL, true or false?

302. After the Tennessee Oilers moved from Houston, where did they settle?

303. When the Tennessee Oilers moved to Nashville, they changed their name to what?

304. Carson Palmer is a native Californian, true or false?

305. Which super bowl did the Chicago Bears first win?

306. The first super bowl Chicago Bears won, it was against which team?

307. Who won the MVP award in Super Bowl XX?

308. In the 1998 season, Kansas City Chiefs had how many penalties?

309. The raiders had how many penalties in the 1996 season?

310. Eric Dickerson led the NFL in 1988 with how many yards?

311. When was Alan Ameche's rookie year?

312. The first team to win the super bowl as a wide card team is?

313. The team that originally drafted John Unitas was?

314. Without throwing a touchdown pass during the game, who was the first quarterback to win the super bowl MVP?

315. Which position did Walter Payton's older brother play?

316. The person that led the NFC in receptions in the 1998 season was?

317. Antonio Freeman has how many receptions in the 1998 season?

318. Frank Sanders had how many receptions in the 1998 season?

319. In college, Bobby Engram wore which number?

320. At what age did Barry Sanders retire?

321. In retirement, how many yards did Barry Sanders have?

322. In the 20th century, which player played 20 seasons with the same team?

323. When was Jackie Slater's first season with the Rams?

324. When was Jackie Slater last swain with the Rams?

325. When was Jackie Slaters inducted into the NFL hall of fame?

326. How many NFL games were seen on Thanksgiving day in 1939?

327. The first team to give up more than 510 points in a season was?

328. How many seasons did Jim Brown spend in the NFL?

329. Jim Brown won how many rushing titles?

330. When was Jim Brown inducted into the NFL hall of fame?

331. In which year did Jim Brown retire?

332. When did the Baltimore Colts give up more than 510 points in a season?

333. The first team in the NFL to be blown out of a gnaw with more than 25 points is?

334. Which position does George Atkinson play?

335. When was Len Ford inducted into the Pro football hall of fame?

336. Which position did Len Ford play for the Cleveland Browns?

337. How many seasons did Len Ford play for the Cleveland Browns?

338. When did Ray Flaherty start to coach the Washington redskins?

339. When did the Detroit Lions win their second NFL championship?

340. Chicago Bears were undefeated in the 1943 regular season, true or false?

341. Which team drafted Michale Vick in 2001?

342. The first super bowl was won by the Green Bay Packers when they beat which team?

343. In the 1990s, who was the only player to have 10 interceptions in a single season?

344. When did the Jacksonville Jaguars join the NFL?

345. When did the Carolina Panthers join the NFL?

346. Deon Sanders began his NFL career with which team?

347. Super Bowl XXIX was played in which city?

348. In week four of the 2002 season, how many receptions did Deion Branch have?

349. Who was the runner-up in the rookie of the year in the 2001 season?

350. Which non-wide receiver caught the most passes in the 1999 season?

351. The USFL franchise that relocated three times in three years was?

352. Which college did Larry Allen attend?

353. The Boston breakers moved to New Orleans in which year?

354. In 2003, Garry Anderson was in his 22nd season, true or false?

355. John Elway played how many AFC championships?

356. The one loss John Elway had in the AFC was against which team?

357. Kordell Stewart's nickname is?

358. How many passer ratings did Peyton Manning have in 2004?

359. Whose passer rating record did Peyton Manning break in 2004?

360. Which team won the NFL championship in 1927?

361. The first regular season game that was played outside the United States was won by which team?

362. The first NFL regular season game that was played outside of the United States was in which place?

363. The first regular season game played outside the United States was in which year?

364. How many points did Indianapolis Colts get in the 1991 season?

365. How many points did the Seahawks score in the 1991 season?

366. Did Jerry Glanville play in the NFL? yes or no?

367. Jerry Glanville was the head coach of which team starting from 1985?

368. The first player in the NFL to compile 200 quarterback sacks in a career was?

369. Which position did Sonny Jurgensen play in?

370. Sonny Jurgensen started his career with which team?

371. How many seasons did Sonny Jurgensen play in the NFL?

372. How many seasons did Sonny Jurgensen play for the Philadelphia eagles?

373. In which year did Sonny Jurgensen retire?

374. When was Sonny Jurgensen inducted into the NFL hall of fame?

375. Ralph Anderson played his rookie season in which year?

376. What did Ralph Anderson die of?

377. The San Diego Chargers lost to which team in the 1961 NFL championship?

378. What was the name of the Washington Redskins before they moved to Washington?

379. The first player that scored a touchdown for the New Orleans Saints was?

380. In 1984, who was the head coach of the Los Angeles Express?

381. How many yards did Emmitt Smith have in the 1995 season?

382. How many yards did Emmitt Smith have in the 1994 season?

383. In 1984, who was the quarterback of the Los Angeles Express?

384. Before the Falcons traded up, which team first picked Michael Vick in the 2001 draft?

385. Which team did the Detroit Lions defeat to win their second NFL championship?

386. Which team won the NFL championship in 1954?

387. Which team won the NFL championship in 1953?

388. The first stadium used by the Green Bay Packers was?

389. What was the final score of the 1963 AFL championship game between the Boston Patriots and the San Diego Chargers?

390. The Chicago Bears went undefeated in the 1934 regular season, true or false?

391. After which season did George Atkinson retire?

392. The fourth NFL coach to take a different team to the super bowl was?

393. Did Dick Vermeil coach the Baltimore Colts in the past? Yes or no?

394. Did Dick Vermeil coach the Philadelphia Eagles in the past? yes or no?

395. When was Ray Flaherty inducted into the Pro football hall of fame?

396. Which club did Jackie Slater play for 20 years?

397. The team that racked up 6288 yards in 1961 was?

398. QB sack became an official NFL statistic in which year?

399. Leslie O'Neal played college football where?

400. How many career touchdowns did Lance Alworth have for the San Diego Chargers?

401. Randall Cunningham was a rookie on which team?

402. In Super Bowl XXXII, Green Bay Packers lost to which team?

403. The real first name of Bo Jackson is?

404. Rich Gannon went to which college?

405. Which team did Rich Gannon play for in 1987?

406. Which team led the NFL in total points in 2000?

407. How many points did Marshall Faulk score in the 2000 NFL season?

408. How many receptions did Terry Glenn catch in one game in his second year in the NFL?

409. Who led the NFL in sacks in the 1982 season?

410. When were sacks first recorded in the NFL?

411. How many yards did Emmitt Smith have in 1993?

412. Which team did Bill Goldbergplau for in the NFL?

413. What was the major thing that stunted Bill Goldberg's career?

414. The team that drafted but never signed Dick Butkus was?

415. How many teams have played at least 4 super bowls?

416. The team that drafted Garrison Hears was?

417. Which position does Edgerrin James play?

418. From 1999 to 2005, how many Edgerrin James rushed how many yards?

419. Edgerrin James played for the Arizona Cardinals from 2006 to?

420. The running that scored 40 points in one game is?

421. The third season Ernie Nevers spent in the NFL was in which year?

422. When did Ernie Nevers retire?

423. Who was the head coach of the Miami Dolphins in 2007?

424. Who was the head coach of the Miami Dolphins in 2008?

425. The first team to score 500 points in a back-to-back season was?

426. How many points did St Louis Rams score in 1999?

427. How many points did St Louis Rams score in 2001?

428. Portsmouth Spartans later became which team in the NFL?

429. Who won the NFL championship in 1935?

430. What was the nickname of Mike Alstott?

431. Which position did Mike Alstott play?

432. How many yards did Mike Alstott rush in his career?

433. When did Mike Alstott retire?

434. The team that had the first quarterback to throw over 1000 yards in a season was?

435. Which position did Arnie Herber play in?

436. Which position did Dan Towler play in?

437. Jim Brown quit his NFL career to start which career?

438. Forrest Gregg was elected into the hall of fame in which year?

439. The head coach when the Philadelphia Eagles won their first NFL championship was?

440. Who won the MVP in super bowl X?

441. Who won the super bowl XXXVI MVP?

442. Which high school did Tom Brady attend?

443. Lance Alworth averaged more than 100 yards for how many consecutive seasons?

444. The first AFL player to be inducted into the hall of fame is?

445. The Washington Redskins had how many losses during Joe Gibbs's first stint as their head coach?

446. The first African-American NFL player was signed in which year?

447. Kenny Washington played for the Los Angeles Rams as?

448. Sammy Baugh played two positions, quarterback and?

449. Anthony Carter played in which position?

450. Bobby Hebert played in which position?

451. The USFL lawsuit against the NFL in 1985 won then how much?

452. How many sacks did Reggie white collect in 1987?

453. Reggie White collected how many sacks in 1988?

454. Buddy Ryan was famous for the 46 defense, true or false?

455. Who took the Pittsburgh Steelers to super bowl XIV?

456. Who coached the Chicago Bears in 1985?

457. The person that led the NFL in passing yards in 1999 was?

458. Marcus Allen was a non-kicker, true or false?

459. The first pick in the 1990 NFL draft was?

460. Who came 2nf overall in the 1990 NFL draft?

461. Who took Jeff George the first overall in the 1990 NFL draft?

462. The first and only USFL rookie of the year was?

463. The University of Oklahoma has won how many national championships?

464. Norm Johnson scored how many points in 1995?

465. Norm Johnson was playing for which club in 1995?

466. Jerome Bettis went to which college?

467. How many picks did Dick Lane have in 1952?

468. The first head coach to win three super bowls was?

469. Which person took the Pittsburgh Steelers to super bowl IX?

470. Chuck Noll retired in which year?

471. How many years did Chuck Noll spend at the Pittsburgh Steelers?

472. On November 23, 1966, Don Meredith hit Bob Hayes with a pass that covered how many yards?

473. In which year were the Falcons outscored 240 to 290 during the season?

474. Which quarterback was the highlight of the Ram's first NFL championship?

475. Who was the head coach of the Cleveland Rams in 1945?

476. When was Bob Waterfield inducted into the NFL hall of fame?

477. The first player to win three NFL super bowl MVP awards was?

478. Which position does Joe Montana play?

479. When Joe Montana won his MVP award, which club was he playing for?

480. The third pick in the 2001 NFL draft was?

481. The playing field will be rimmed by a solid white border how many feet wide along the end lines and sidelines?

482. The game shall be played upon a rectangular field, 360 feet in length, and how many feet wide?

483. The Field includes the Field of Play and what zones?

484. The areas bounded by goal lines, end lines, and sidelines on NFL field are known as?

485. What is the full meaning of OR in the NFL?

486. What is the full meaning of AR in the NFL?

487. What is a ruling made in the interim between the annual rules meetings that is only official during the current season?

488. A Dead Ball is one that is not in which place?

489. What is a written decision on a given statement of facts and serves to illustrate the application of a rule?

490. Which ruling in the NFL is also used to indicate pertinent references to other rules?

491. Any act, other than passing or successful handing which results in a loss of player possession is known as?

492. Any live ball that is not in player possession is known as?

493. The touching of a loose ball by a player in an unsuccessful attempt to collect it is known as?

494. When a player intentionally contacts an eligible receiver who is in front of a defender, what is it called?

495. Provided an opponent is not a runner, blocking from behind below the wait is called what?

496. The intentional striking of a ball with any part of the hand is called what?

497. The rectangle formed by the goal lines and sidelines is known as.

498. A foul that occurs after the snap until the ball of the dead is known as?

499. If not permitted, handing the ball forward to a teammate is illegal. True or False?

500. A player is not offside if any part of his body is outside the neural zone, true or false?

501. NFL professional games are how many hours long?

502. The NFL game is divided into how many quarters?

503. Each quarter consists of how many minutes?

504. In each half, each team is entitled to how many timeouts?

505. What is another name for extra time in the NFL?

506. The rules of overtime changed in the 2016-17 season, True or False?

507. The first super bowl to get overtime was?

508. The 2019 NFC and AFC championship games both went overtime, true or false?

509. There is a dead ball when a team scores, True or False?

510. There is no Deadball when a touchback occurs, True or False?

511. The second owner of the Seattle Seahawks was?

512. The first NFL season the Atlanta Falcons played was in which year?

513. Atlanta Falcons first won their division title in which year?

514. The Atlanta Falcons finished the 1071 season with a record of 8 wins, 6 losses, and how many ties?

515. Jerry Rice caught his last NFL pass on which team?

516. Which position did Franco Harris play?

517. When did Jerry Rice join the Raiders?

518. How many hands did Jerry Rice get for Oakland in 2004?

519. Which position does Corey Dillon play?

520. How many yards did Corey Dillon rush against the Denver Broncos in 2000?

521. How many super bowl rings does Corey Dillon have?

522. The team that won the first world bowl was?

523. The Cardinals can trace their history back to which year?

524. Gale Sayers entered the NFL in which year?

525. The first club Gale Sayers played for in the NFL was?

526. Which position did Gale Sayers play in?

527. What was the nickname of Gale Sayers?

528. Who led the league in rushing in 1958?

529. The famous retired NFL player that promoted the XFL was?

530. Jim Kelly has thrown four interceptions in a super bowl game, true or false?

531. Which team was Norm Johnson playing for in 1987?

532. How many super bowls has Steve Young won as a starter?

533. Herman Moore made how many touchdowns on turf in 1993?

534. Which shirt number does Tom Brady wear?

535. Which team did Roger Staubach play for in 1977?

536. Kenny Stabler wore which number with the Raiders?

537. Sonny Jurgensen wore which number for the Redskins?

538. What is the name of the mascot of the University of Arkansas Monticello?

539. In 1978, the Tampa Bay Buccaneers were outscored with how many points?

540. How many games did the Tampa Bay Buccaneers lose in 1978?

541. OJ Simpson played 11 seasons between the Bills and which other club?

542. The first head coach to win 300 games in his career was?

543. George Halas coached from 1920 to which year?

544. The second head coach in the NFL to win 300 games in their career was?

545. The Seattle Seahawks became an NFL expansion team in which year?

546. Which position does Jim Zorn play?

547. The Tampa Bay Buccaneers became an expansion team in which year?

548. The second football stadium used by the Houston Oilers was?

549. Dick Butkus was one of the chairmen of the XFL, true or false?

550. Which shirt number does Aaron Roger wear?

Answers to American Football Trivia Questions

1.   Los Angeles

2.   San Diego

3.   2

4.   1

5.   Hard Rock Stadium

6.   Ed Hochuli

7.   Super Bowl XXVII

8.   1963

9.   120 yards.

10.   2003

11.   1961

12.   Miami Dolphins

13.   George Wilson

14.   Cincinnati

15.   2006

16.   Quarterback

17.   49ers

18.   South

19.   Tampa Bay Buccaneers

20. 4

21. Tom Brady

22. Cardinals

23. Ohio

24. Colts

25. Adrien Peterson

26. Miami Dolphins

27. one

28. Oakland

29. Cowboys Stadium

30. Texas Tech University

31. Chargers

32. David Tyree

33. 8

34. Chiefs

35. Tom Brady

36. Quarterback

37. 1

38. Chicago

39. Browns

40. 9

41. D.T

42.   Panthers

43.   Tim Couch

44.   Indianapolis Colts

45.   Cowboys

46.   1982

47.   Eagles

48.   Arizona Cardinals

49.   Tampa

50.   1988

51.   Sam Bradford

52.   Eric Dickerson

53.   Tulane Stadium

54.   2013

55.   Adam Vinatieri

56.   AT&T Stadium

57.   NRG Stadium

58.   Wide receiver

59.   16

60.   Green Bay Packers

61.   47 yards

62.   2013

63.   160 feet (53 1/3 yards)

64.   Pasadena

65.   Metlife stadium

66.   Pittsburgh Steelers

67.   New Orleans

68.   Wide receiver

69.   Leon Lett.

70.   Lamar Hunt

71.   The law firm

72.   True

73.   Quakers

74.   Gunslinger

75.   Quarterback

76.   Detroit

77.   New Orleans

78.   John Fox

79.   Adam Vinatieri

80.   Wide receiver

81.   Atlanta

82.   1996

83.   Wide receiver

84.   False

85.   New York City

86.   St Louis Rams

87.   Bruce Arians

88.   13

89.   Houston

90.   Jacksonville

91.   Cliff Avril

92.   Running back

93.   2011

94.   Thomas

95.   Running back

96.   Bill Belichick

97.   1964

98.   2013

99.   Jim Thorpe

100.   Three

101.   11

102.   New Orleans

103.   Gary Kubiak

104.   Los Angeles

105.   New Orleans

106.   Cardinals

107.   Indianapolis

108.   Saints

109.   Quarterback

110.   101

111.   John Dorsey

112.   1996

113.   Pasadena

114.   East Rutherford

115.   1966

116.   Green Bay Packers

117.   True

118.   Broncos

119.   The Bills

120.   True

121.   True

122.   1929

123.   2010

124.   Washington Redskins

125.   222

126.   New England Patriots

127.   Canton Bulldogs

128.   Tampa Bay Buccaneers

129.   1920

130. 2007

131. 1926

132. Don Shula

133. George Wilson

134. True

135. 15 years

136. 26 years

137. Doug Williams

138. True

139. Buccaneers

140. Los Angeles memorial coliseum

141. Massachusetts

142. 1968

143. 2000

144. Earl Curley

145. Gene Ronzani

146. The Vikings

147. 1921

148. Running back

149. Philadelphia Eagles

150. Linebacker

151. Linebacker

152.   11

153.   Shaun Alexander

154.   Curtis Martin

155.   Baltimore Ravens

156.   Three super bowls

157.   Washington Redskins

158.   Yes

159.   True

160.   Garo Yepremian

161.   Miami Dolphins

162.   Yes

163.   Detroit Lions

164.   True

165.   Kicker

166.   Buffalo Bills

167.   No

168.   True

169.   1982

170.   Oklahoma

171.   6538 yards

172.   Pittsburgh Steelers

173.   Dalla cowboys

174. 58-yard reverse

175. 141.5 sacks

176. 160 sacks

177. 1960

178. 198 sacks

179. 200 sacks

180. Four seasons

181. 9 games

182. John Carney

183. 8

184. 1964

185. 2010

186. 513 points

187. Houston Oilers

188. Kicker

189. Hines Ward

190. Frank Youell Field

191. True

192. Super Bowl XXXVIII

193. Quarterback

194. FedEx Field

195. 6 times

196.   Lou Groza

197.   Falcons

198.   91,704

199.   13 games

200.   55

201.   32

202.   Yes

203.   True

204.   Marcus Allen

205.   RB

206.   True

207.   16

208.   Running back

209.   Roger Craig

210.   London Monarchs

211.   49ers

212.   NFL Europe

213.   Chuck Howley

214.   True

215.   Atlanta Falcons

216.   True

217.   False

218. Denver Broncos

219. Safeties

220. True

221. Cleveland

222. 2004

223. Art Monk

224. Cleveland Browns

225. 2001

226. True

227. New Orleans saints

228. Toes on his right foot

229. 6

230. 1920

231. John McKay

232. 2001

233. 1983 draft

234. Bruce Smith

235. AFC west

236. True

237. False

238. True

239. 1959

240. Two

241. LA Xtreme

242. 492

243. 245 yards

244. True

245. Akron Pros

246. 1926

247. 1995

248. Chicago Bears

249. 1997

250. 2010

251. 1922

252. 1960

253. University of Tennessee

254. Quarterback

255. Chicago Bears

256. 21 years

257. 274

258. True

259. Pottsville Maroons

260. The Rams

261. 1943

262.   11

263.   Charles Haley

264.   49ers

265.   1999

266.   2004 Kansas City Chiefs

267.   483 points

268.   435

269.   True

270.   San Diego Chargers

271.   1973

272.   6 years in 1979

273.   Alan page

274.   1971

275.   1974

276.   Don Shula

277.   Don Shula

278.   1976

279.   False

280.   Dewayne Robertson

281.   Defensive tackle

282.   Carolina Panthers

283.   Mushin Muhammad

284.   Los Angeles Rams

285.   1950

286.   True

287.   Quarterback

288.   1968

289.   1972

290.   True

291.   False

292.   Brett Favre

293.   15 seasons

294.   Punter

295.   Brooklyn Tigers

296.   14

297.   Leroy Andrews

298.   1925

299.   Frankie Albert

300.   Yankee Stadium

301.   True

302.   Memphis

303.   Titans

304.   True

305.   Super Bowl XX

306. New Orleans Patriots

307. Richard Dent

308. 158

309. 156 penalties

310. 1659 yards

311. 1955

312. Oakland Raiders

313. Pittsburgh Steelers

314. Joe Namath

315. Running back

316. Frank Sanders

317. 84

318. 89

319. 10

320. 30 years

321. 15,269 yards

322. Jackie Slater

323. 1976

324. 1995

325. 2001

326. one

327. Baltimore Colts

328. 9 seasons

329. 8

330. 1971

331. 1965

332. 1981

333. Washington redskins

334. Defensive back

335. 1976

336. Defensive end

337. 1950 to 1957

338. 1936

339. 1952

340. True

341. Falcons

342. Kansas City

343. Mark Carrier

344. 1995

345. 1995

346. Atlanta Falcons

347. Miami

348. 13

349. LaDainian Tomlinson

350. Marshall Faulk

351. Breakers

352. Sonoma State

353. 1984

354. True

355. 6

356. Buffalo Bills

357. Slash

358. 121.1

359. Steve Young

360. New York Giants

361. Arizona Cardinals

362. Mexico

363. 2005

364. 143 points

365. 140

366. No

367. Oilers

368. Reggie White

369. Quarterback

370. Philadelphia Eagles

371. 18 seasons.

372. 7

373. 1974

374. 1983

375. 1958

376. Diabetes attack

377. Oilers

378. Boston redskins

379. John Gilliam

380. John Hadl

381. 1773 yards

382. 1484 yards

383. Steve Young

384. Chargers

385. Cleveland browns

386. Cleveland browns

387. Detroit Lions

388. Hagemeister Park

389. Chargers 51 and Patriots 10

390. True

391. 1979

392. Dick Vermeil

393. Yes

394. NO

395. 1976

396. Rams

397. Houston Oilers

398. 1982

399. Oklahoma State

400. 83

401. Philadelphia Eagles

402. Denver Broncos

403. Vincent

404. Delaware

405. Vikings

406. Marshall Faulk

407. 160 points

408. 13 receptions

409. Doug Martins

410. 1982

411. 1486 yards

412. Sacramento Surge

413. Injuries

414. Denver Broncos

415. 11

416. Cardinals

417. Running back

418. 9226 yards

419. 2008

420. Ernie Nevers

421. 1926

422. 1931

423. Cam Cameron

424. Tony Sparano

425. St Louis Rams

426. 526 Rams

427. 503

428. Detroit Lions

429. Detroit Lions

430. A-train

431. Fullback

432. 5088 yards

433. 2006

434. Green Bay Packers

435. Quarterback

436. Fullback

437. Acting

438. 1977

439. Earle Neale

440. Lynn Swann

441. Tom Brady

442. Junipero Serra High School

443. 3

444. Lance Alworth

445. 1

446. 1946

447. Halfback

448. Defensive back

449. Wide receiver

450. Quarterback

451. $1

452. 21

453. 18

454. True

455. Chuck Noll

456. Buddy Ryan

457. Steve Beuerlein

458. True

459. Jeff George

460.   Kennedy by Seahawks

461.   Baltimore Colts

462.   Jim Kelly.

463.   7

464.   141

465.   Pittsburgh Steelers

466.   Notre Dome

467.   14

468.   Chuck Noll

469.   Chuck Noll

470.   1991

471.   23 years

472.   83 yards

473.   1978

474.   Bob Waterfield

475.   Adam Walsh

476.   1965

477.   Joe Montana

478.   Quarterback

479.   49ers

480.   Gerrard Warren

481.   6 feet

482. 160 feet

483. End zones

484. End zones

485. Official Ruling

486. Approved ruling

487. Official Ruling

488. In play

489. Approved ruling

490. Approved ruling

491. Fumble

492. Loose ball

493. Muff

494. Chucking

495. Clipping

496. Bat

497. Field of play.

498. A live ball foul

499. True

500. False

501. 1 hour

502. 4

503. 15

504.   3

505.   Overtime

506.   True

507.   Super Bowl LI

508.   True

509.   True

510.   False

511.   Ken Behring

512.   1966

513.   1980

514.   1

515.   Seattle Seahawks

516.   Running back

517.   2001

518.   4 Hanes

519.   Running back

520.   278 yards

521.   1

522.   Birmingham Americans

523.   1898

524.   1965

525.   Chicago Bears

526. Running back

527. The Kansas comet

528. Jim Brown

529. Dick Butkus

530. True

531. Seattle Seahawks

532. 1

533. 6

534. 12

535. Dallas Cowboys

536. 12

537. 9

538. Bill Weevil

539. 287

540. All regular season games

541. 49ers

542. George Halas

543. 1967

544. Don Shula

545. 1976

546. Quarterback

547. 1976

548.   Rice Stadium

549.   True

550.   12

WELCOME TO
WORD SEARCH PUZZLES SECTION

INTRODUCTION

- This word search puzzle is created around the interest football terms and slangs. It is created to help football lover have hours of fun searching for football related words.

- **HOW TO SOLVE**

- Find all the word capitalized word listed below the word search grid on each page. Words are hidden in the grids of the puzzle in straight, unbroken lines: forward, backwards, up, down or diagonal. Words can over lap and cross each other. When you find a word, circle it in the grid and mark the word in the list so you will know it has been found. Each words should be searched for as individual word.

- **EASY TO CUT OUT**

- This book has wide inner margins, this will make it easy to cut out the page and take them with you as some people find this method convenient.

- **SPECIAL REQUEST**

- Please leave a brief honest review about this book on amazon.com. It will really be helpful. Thanks

PUZZLE 1

```
C A R D I N A L S M Q O
F I E L D O F P L A Y D
B B U O I Q D G K X H E
O U B G H R O C P O T
B C C I X G O A H R R R
V C V F I H P L O O S O
X A Z E W M K P P T E I
X N Z I E A I O B E C T
Y E X 4 Q R C S L C O L
R E F 9 R Y K T O T L I
J R F E C L T S C Q L O
B S P R E A D P K C A N
A A N S E N Z J L Z R S
F I R S T D O W N N S J
```

CARDINALS
MAXPROTECT
SEATTLE
49ERS
GOALPOSTS
SPREAD

DETROITLIONS
FIELDOFPLAY
DROPKICK
VEER
HORSECOLLAR

HOOK
CHOPBLOCK
BUCCANEERS
FIRSTDOWN
MARYLAND

PUZZLE 2

```
J  Z  O  N  E  R  E  A  D  T  A  Z
G  O  M  N  N  S  E  R  I  E  S  M
E  M  U  C  C  P  C  D  A  I  Q  M
E  R  F  O  R  L  H  B  F  N  F  U
E  S  F  P  O  A  I  G  U  L  L  V
G  Q  E  T  A  Y  C  B  L  M  A  H
I  U  D  I  C  A  A  K  L  I  G  G
U  I  P  O  H  C  G  I  B  H  X  P
A  B  U  N  M  T  O  C  A  A  H  J
D  K  N  R  E  I  B  K  C  N  C  F
M  I  T  U  N  O  E  O  K  D  O  K
M  C  G  N  T  N  A  F  J  O  M  V
Q  K  Y  B  R  U  R  F  W  F  W  B
X  N  B  X  T  C  S  T  U  F  F  O
```

KICKOFF
ENCROACHMENT
CHICAGOBEARS
SERIES
ZONEREAD
MUFFEDPUNT

PLAYACTION
OPTIONRUN
STUFF
DIG
CRACKBACK

HANDOFF
FULLBACK
FLAG
REDFLAG
SQUIBKICK

PUZZLE 3

```
W  I  L  L  T  I  T  A  N  S  N  H
I  N  O  E  U  N  T  Y  P  C  E  A
M  T  S  I  I  T  H  A  M  R  U  I
O  E  A  J  N  Z  R  S  A  E  T  L
I  R  N  H  T  U  E  U  R  E  R  M
D  C  G  M  E  N  E  K  T  N  A  A
N  E  E  A  R  B  P  X  Y  P  L  R
L  P  L  N  F  A  O  N  B  A  Z  Y
Q  T  E  R  E  L  I  S  A  S  O  H
P  I  S  O  R  A  N  K  L  S  N  R
T  O  R  S  E  N  T  C  L  O  E  Y
W  N  A  T  N  C  I  D  A  K  T  D
G  Y  M  E  C  E  H  W  I  A  J  U
T  U  S  R  E  D  S  H  I  R  T  K
```

LOSANGELESRAMS   NCAA   INTERCEPTION
NEUTRALZONE   TITANS   SLOT
UNBALANCED   REDSHIRT   MARTYBALL
WILL   INTERFERENCE MANROSTER
SCREENPASS   HIKE   THREEPOINT
HAILMARY

81

PUZZLE 4

```
B  U  S  T  E  D  P  L  A  Y  R  M
D  S  I  D  E  Z  O  N  E  E  A  Z
P  C  G  M  Y  T  Z  M  U  E  P  P
P  R  T  R  H  C  G  Z  T  U  Q  O
L  I  H  T  P  J  U  T  Y  Q  U  S
F  M  N  F  L  E  U  R  O  P  A  S
T  M  B  A  Z  O  R  S  M  V  R  E
Y  A  R  D  C  U  F  J  N  I  T  S
A  G  C  S  H  O  Q  F  A  K  E  S
I  E  S  T  R  I  N  G  E  I  R  I
F  O  U  R  T  H  D  O  W  N  J  O
S  T  I  F  F  A  R  M  K  G  S  N
E  H  A  S  H  M  A  R  K  S  B  E
R  E  S  T  R  A  I  N  I  N  G  V
```

HURRYUP	SCRIMMAGE	SCOUTTEAM
QUARTER	POSSESSION	BUSTEDPLAY
NFLEUROPA	RESTRAINING	YARD
HASHMARKS	STRING	SIDEZONE
STIFFARM	OFFENSE	FOURTHDOWN
VIKINGS		

PUZZLE 5

```
L E G W H I P L W A O P
Z X I B F R A U X E B H
D D F U I R S P N A U I
G U L T E Y S B C T B L
Z C E T L I A A P X B A
O M A O D B T C K J L D
A L F N G U T K B U E E
P E L H O X E M O M S L
Q I I O A T M X O B C P
H G C O L Y P Z T O R H
M W K K P T T A L F E I
Y K E L Z U P V E J E A
Q J R L S H O T G U N Z
Z B L A C K M O N D A Y
```

UPBACK
JUMBO
PASSATTEMPT
BUBBLESCREEN
BUTTONHOOK
PHILADELPHIA

LATERAL
PICK
FLEAFLICKER
BLACKMONDAY
BOOTLEG

PAT
LEGWHIP
FIELDGOAL
PUNT
SHOTGUN

83

PUZZLE 6

```
M G B I T J L K G N C O
R E A L P A S R P O H D
I N C L Q C N P W S A Z
B D K E U K E I X E M F
P A F G I O A T R T P A
F R I A C M K T A A I L
V O E L K A O S I C O S
U U L M K H C B D K N E
T N D O I K A U E L S S
D D E T C I O R R E H T
M O E I K H O G S I I A
T G W O Y Y P H K T P R
C O R N E R B A C K D T
Q U A R T E R B A C K C
```

SNEAK
QUARTERBACK
FALSESTART
CORNERBACK
PITTSBURGH
RPO

HOTREAD
BACKFIELD
ENDAROUND
DOWN
RAIDERS

QUICKKICK
NOSETACKLE
ILLEGALMOTION
CHAMPIONSHIP
JACK

PUZZLE 7

```
P  J  N  G  J  P  B  O  X  G  T  F
S  M  N  F  K  H  Z  S  X  E  R  X
K  I  E  P  W  U  R  U  S  H  K  Y
R  A  W  I  I  Y  C  O  X  C  Z  E
G  M  Y  S  D  H  R  S  A  H  F  L
T  I  O  T  E  P  E  B  T  E  I  L
N  D  R  O  R  F  T  A  O  C  E  O
B  O  K  L  E  A  U  L  U  K  L  W
K  L  G  S  C  T  R  T  C  D  D  F
C  P  I  S  E  T  N  I  H  O  J  L
C  H  A  T  I  E  H  M  D  W  U  A
Z  I  N  R  V  M  P  O  O  N  D  G
A  N  T  I  E  P  Q  R  W  S  G  K
K  S  S  P  R  T  T  E  N  P  E  V
```

PISTOL
ATTEMPT
CHECKDOWN   RUSH   MIAMIDOLPHINS
RETURN   NEWYORKGIANTS   STRIP
WIDERECEIVER   BALTIMORE   SCATBACK
BOX   PROSET   YELLOWFLAG
                    TOUCHDOWN   FIELDJUDGE

PUZZLE 8

```
F  R  E  E  P  L  A  Y  T  I  F  J
O  U  Y  B  F  W  S  B  O  F  U  A
T  I  A  Q  N  C  I  A  U  R  D  C
T  A  R  G  E  T  N  L  C  M  E  K
G  R  D  Y  W  B  G  L  H  F  F  S
A  X  A  J  Y  Z  L  C  B  L  E  O
P  K  G  P  O  V  E  O  A  A  N  N
Z  O  E  D  R  F  W  N  C  N  S  V
A  N  C  I  K  G  I  T  K  K  I  I
B  N  G  K  J  G  N  R  R  E  V  L
G  U  N  N  E  R  G  O  U  R  E  L
X  O  V  G  T  T  W  L  A  F  E  E
W  M  O  N  S  T  E  R  M  A  N  I
E  B  T  U  R  N  O  V  E  R  D  Q
```

TRAP
BALLCONTROL
TOUCHBACK
POCKET
BLOCK
FREEPLAY

TURNOVER
YARDAGE
MONSTERMAN
JACKSONVILLE
DEFENSIVEEND

NEWYORKJETS
TARGET
SINGLEWING
FLANKER

PUZZLE 9

```
B  R  F  Z  T  F  D  C  F  X  D  A
O  U  I  L  Y  I  L  W  Y  R  S  G
O  N  F  A  E  L  W  A  C  E  W  F
E  N  B  F  F  X  L  M  T  C  R  Q
P  R  S  N  A  P  B  Z  M  E  U  K
B  O  K  I  K  L  J  O  T  I  S  S
S  V  I  C  D  C  O  N  N  V  P  L
I  E  I  I  O  E  U  B  N  E  I  O
E  R  M  A  H  P  K  B  I  R  R  W
T  B  P  I  G  S  K  I  N  L  A  M
W  P  L  A  Y  C  L  O  C  K  L  E
B  Q  K  K  L  Z  G  Q  M  K  X  S
G  N  M  I  N  N  E  S  O  T  A  H
N  F  O  R  W  A  R  D  P  A  S  S
```

NFL
PLAYCLOCK
FORWARDPASS
SNAP
ONSIDEKICK
FLEXBONE

SLOWMESH
ROVER
MINNESOTA
PIGSKIN
XRECEIVER

SPIRAL
TRICKPLAY
FLAT
PUNTER
BUFFALOBILLS

PUZZLE 10

```
M X W C L E V E L A N D
O S E C O N D A R Y F V
P A S S B D E G E K A S
Z E A F H P A O C W I U
N X N F C H D A B A R C
J T F W O A B L T S C C
X R R A V L A L W H A E
T A A L E F L I C I T S
I P N K R B L N H N C S
D O C O Y A R E I G H F
D I I N F C C R E T K U
N N S A H K P O F O I L
C T C G O S R Q S N C L
W N O N J S M G H W K Y
```

GOALLINE   CHIEFS   WALKON
SECONDARY   NICKELBACK   SUCCESSFULLY
CLEVELAND   HALFBACK   COVER
EXTRAPOINT   DEADBALL   PASS
FAIRCATCHKICK   SPRINT   SANFRANCISCO
WASHINGTON

PUZZLE 11

```
P O S T P A T T E R N L
I N C O M P L E T E C O
D S T U N T F X X V K N
C H A R G E R S V W Q G
K I G U I J A G U A R S
O F J N C P L O P Z A N
U T Y P O X S L S H U A
L T E A M M A T E K K P
G R A S P I N G R L I P
O P S S L W C L Q C C E
Y Q S J E G E K V I K R
M B V A T L A N T A L S
Y J X D E C D Q W L L G
N E W O R L E A N S J W
```

OSKIE	CHARGERS	COMPLETE
SHIFT	TEAMMATE	JAGUARS
TRIPS	KICK	POSTPATTERN
NEWORLEANS	GRASPING	ATLANTA
RUNPASS	INCOMPLETE	LONGSNAPPER
STUNT		

PUZZLE 12

```
I  N  D  I  R  E  C  T  S  N  A  P
G  M  C  P  I  B  S  A  M  J  S  N
W  A  I  M  L  E  D  A  V  G  N  D
X  N  T  K  L  G  S  P  I  K  E  Y
M  O  A  B  E  Z  P  K  T  F  W  J
Z  E  M  Y  G  F  E  I  K  B  E  Z
U  U  P  E  A  J  C  C  B  I  N  O
F  V  A  A  L  U  I  K  A  J  G  N
G  R  B  L  S  K  A  S  G  M  L  E
W  E  A  O  H  E  L  I  I  S  A  B
L  I  Y  C  I  B  J  X  E  K  N  L
I  W  O  Y  F  O  R  W  A  R  D  I
V  O  E  S  T  D  B  T  Q  C  N  T
P  L  A  C  E  K  I  C  K  Z  P  Z
```

NEWENGLAND   **FUMBLE**   **MIKE**
SPIKE   **JUKE**   **FORWARD**
PLACEKICK   **ZONEBLITZ**   **POOCHKICK**
SAM   **ILLEGALSHIFT**   **TAMPABAY**
MANOEUVRE   **SPECIAL**   **KICKSIX**
INDIRECTSNAP

PUZZLE 13

```
E  V  E  Y  J  F  G  A  C  C  W  D
I  M  A  M  I  I  R  B  O  U  A  A
T  A  C  K  L  E  E  A  F  T  O  L
A  U  D  I  B  L  E  L  F  B  Y  L
M  S  C  J  N  D  N  L  I  L  D  A
S  C  R  Z  L  P  B  C  N  O  O  S
F  R  O  J  T  O  A  A  C  C  U  C
A  A  S  U  D  S  Y  R  O  K  B  O
P  M  S  P  N  I  Q  R  R  I  L  W
I  B  B  M  V  T  V  I  N  N  E  B
U  L  A  A  I  I  E  E  E  G  W  O
R  E  R  N  G  O  C  R  R  F  I  Y
C  I  N  C  I  N  N  A  T  I  N  S
S  C  V  W  I  L  D  C  A  T  G  L
```

COFFINCORNER
DALLASCOWBOYS
CROSSBAR
SCRAMBLE
FIELDPOSITION
DOUBLEWING

CUTBLOCKING
CINCINNATI
BALLCARRIER
GREENBAY
WILDCAT

AUDIBLE
DIVE
TACKLE
COUNTER
UPMAN

PUZZLE 14

```
Y S X F M O V E K L F S
S M Z M K K D H L M W F
C A R O L I N A Y A F U
P S K L S U B L G N N M
L H B F T E O O A I F B
H M F S V C P V T N O L
H O F I M E P I E M R E
W U L G B N O O D O M R
T T D D J T N L R T A O
D H J D E E E A I I T O
P N R E L R N T V O I S
G V I J A E T I E N O K
R Z N F A L C O N S N I
J P S C O R I N G W Z J
```

HOLDER
CAROLINA
HUDDLE
MANINMOTION
FALCONS
HALOVIOLATION

OPPONENT
FUMBLEROOSKI
LIVEBALL
FORMATION
SMASHMOUTH

GATEDRIVEN
CENTER
SCORING
OFFSIDE
MOVE

PUZZLE 15

```
X  F  G  F  I  N  B  O  U  N  D  S
D  B  M  P  X  H  P  C  H  P  O  F
L  B  H  A  T  Y  O  O  E  U  U  A
P  I  E  C  F  I  O  C  A  L  B  C
M  K  N  K  A  I  O  R  D  L  L  E
K  N  E  E  L  Q  R  V  C  I  E  M
I  F  O  R  M  A  T  I  O  N  R  A
D  B  B  S  R  A  G  U  A  G  E  S
G  K  C  H  A  I  N  B  C  Z  V  K
F  A  I  R  C  A  T  C  H  M  E  L
B  Q  C  O  M  M  A  N  D  E  R  S
B  A  C  K  W  A  R  D  P  A  S  S
O  X  L  I  N  E  B  A  C  K  E  R
V  R  U  N  N  I  N  G  B  A  C  K
```

LINEMAN
FACEMASK
RUNNINGBACK
FAIRCATCH
PULLING
HEADCOACH

IFORMATION
DOUBLEREVERSE
INBOUNDS
PACKERS
BACKWARDPASS

COMMANDERS
KNEEL
CHAIN
LINEBACKER

93

PUZZLE 16

```
A  S  P  P  U  M  P  F  A  K  E  E
J  T  F  D  R  A  W  P  L  A  Y  Q
R  E  S  P  L  I  T  E  N  D  G  M
M  E  L  R  E  D  Z  O  N  E  A  I
E  L  A  D  M  G  Z  B  C  E  B  Y
I  E  N  F  Z  I  A  W  T  X  U  P
G  R  T  S  R  P  F  L  V  J  S  L
H  S  K  A  N  S  A  S  C  I  T  Y
O  V  E  R  T  I  M  E  F  D  E  O
G  A  I  R  C  O  R  Y  E  L  L  S
S  U  P  E  R  B  O  W  L  G  P  Z
Z  L  P  Q  L  A  S  V  E  G  A  S
U  S  T  A  R  T  E  R  C  T  P  S
L  O  T  E  N  N  E  S  S  E  E  W
```

AIRCORYELL
OVERTIME
BUST
ARIZONA
SPECIALTEAM
DRAWPLAY

PUMPFAKE
SPLITEND
STEELERS
TENNESSEE
REDZONE

SLANT
KANSASCITY
STARTER
LASVEGAS
SUPERBOWL

94

PUZZLE 17

```
P  Z  B  L  I  T  Z  A  T  Z  D  H
N  R  I  U  E  A  I  P  I  H  E  O
E  E  T  W  B  I  Q  F  G  A  F  U
Z  C  A  R  G  L  H  K  H  N  E  S
S  E  J  G  F  B  C  T  T  D  N  T
C  I  I  O  E  A  G  L  E  S  S  O
X  V  Z  K  S  C  R  K  N  T  I  N
S  E  G  Y  J  K  I  I  D  E  V  T
S  R  T  T  P  R  D  C  U  A  E  E
K  U  W  E  A  K  I  K  I  M  B  X
H  G  O  A  L  A  R  E  A  R  A  A
G  U  Q  H  S  Y  O  R  C  J  C  N
C  L  I  P  P  I  N  G  R  B  K  S
I  N  D  I  A  N  A  P  O  L  I  S
```

GOALAREA
CLIPPING
TAILBACK
WEAKI
HANDSTEAM
EAGLES

SACK
HUT
BLITZ
INDIANAPOLIS
DEFENSIVEBACK

GRIDIRON
HOUSTONTEXANS
KICKER
ZRECEIVER
TIGHTEND

PUZZLE 18

```
B L O C K I N G S L E D
D R I V E N Y T W Y I P
F N B L J V A K I I H X
B Z D I R E C T S N A P
L P B A D A Y F H J R E
F A R H B A C K B U D X
R T L E S O I S O R C T
N R M T C Y H A N E O R
U I L C V E F I E D U A
D O K M M H P N Y W N T
C T W S P L I T T H T I
C S Y N Z B R S I Y J M
A G N V I L R V I O J E
R E V E R S E Z B H N G
```

EXTRATIME

YAC

RECEPTION

PATRIOTS

SAINTS

COLTS

WISHBONE

REVERSE

DRIVE

HARDCOUNT

DIRECTSNAP

BLOCKINGSLED

SPLITT

INJURED

HBACK

DIMEBACK

PUZZLE 19

```
S  T  D  O  A  N  S  X  E  T  Q  F
C  O  N  T  A  I  N  P  O  I  M  A
E  N  D  Z  O  N  E  H  L  C  R  N
H  D  E  F  E  N  S  E  X  A  F  T
N  F  J  C  X  P  K  U  W  R  Y  A
P  A  S  S  I  N  G  Y  A  R  D  S
X  C  C  H  A  B  F  E  I  Y  B  Y
F  H  C  B  N  B  X  B  V  F  U  J
S  J  Y  Q  B  M  S  R  E  B  J  P
U  L  Q  L  Z  L  W  Y  D  O  H  X
T  R  U  E  F  R  E  S  H  M  A  N
P  A  C  K  A  G  E  W  B  B  M  Z
M  M  T  Y  I  H  P  Z  P  J  V  L
D  S  E  A  H  A  W  K  S  M  Z  Y
```

FBS
CARRY
ENDZONE
DEFENSE
CONTAIN
SEAHAWKS

SWEEP
PLAY
CHIPSHOT
WAIVED
PACKAGE

PASSINGYARDS
FANTASY
BOMB
FCS
TRUEFRESHMAN

PUZZLE 20

```
F R E E S A F E T Y W V
N S S U A B S N R D F P
I U V L P A N T H E R S
H U M A N T O M A N N D
H O L D I N G K L V Q V
D X J P A N C A K E B O
A S K V I I V X S R B P
K G N C K W O H H B E P
C U I E R B D S O R N O
J A E R N A I A O O G S
B R O W N S V F T N A I
F D O P G K L E I C L N
X D V C S F O T N O S G
E S E Y F A J Y G S V I
```

FREEKICK
PANCAKE
BENGALS
SHOOTING
PANTHERS
RAVENS

BROWNS
GUARD
DOWNBOX
FREESAFETY
OPPOSING

MANTOMAN
ICING
SAFETY
TRY
HOLDING
DENVERBRONCOS

SOLUTION 1

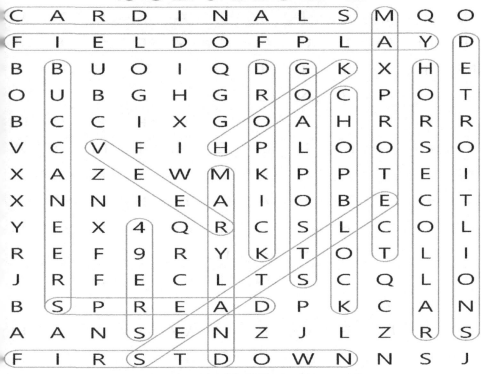

```
C A R D I N A L S M Q O
F I E L D O F P L A Y D
B B U O I Q D G K X H E
O U B G H G R O C P O T
B C C I X G O A H R R R
V C V F I H P L O O S O
X A Z E W M K P P T E I
X N N I E A I O B E C T
Y E X 4 Q R C S L C O L
R E F 9 R Y K T O L L I
J R F E C L T S C Q L O
B S P R E A D P K C A N
A A N S E N Z J L Z R S
F I R S T D O W N N S J
```

SOLUTION 2

```
J Z O N E R E A D T A Z
G O M N N S E R I E S M
E M U N C P C D A I Q M
E R F O R L H B F N F U
E S F P O A I G U L L V
G Q E T A Y C B L M A H
I U D I C A A K L I G G
U I P O H C A G I B H X P
A B U N M C G I B H A H J
D K N R E I B C A N C F
M I T U N T O E O K D O K
M C G N T N B A F J O M V
Q K Y B R U R F F W F W B
X N B X T C S T U F F O
```

99

SOLUTION 3

```
W  I  L  L  T  I  T  A  N  S  N  H
I  N  O  E  U  N  T  Y  P  C  E  A
M  T  S  I  I  T  H  A  M  R  U  I
O  E  A  J  N  Z  R  S  A  R  T  L
I  R  N  H  T  U  E  U  R  E  R  M
D  C  G  M  E  N  E  K  T  N  A  A
N  E  E  A  R  B  P  X  Y  P  L  R
L  P  L  N  F  A  O  N  B  A  Z  Y
Q  T  E  R  E  L  I  S  A  S  O  H
P  I  S  O  R  A  N  K  L  S  N  R
T  O  R  S  E  N  T  C  L  O  E  Y
W  N  A  T  N  C  I  D  A  K  T  D
G  Y  M  E  C  E  H  W  I  A  J  U
T  U  S  R  E  D  S  H  I  R  T  K
```

SOLUTION 4

```
B  U  S  T  E  D  P  L  A  Y  R  M
D  S  I  D  E  Z  O  N  E  E  A  Z
P  C  G  M  Y  T  Z  M  U  E  P  P
P  R  T  R  H  C  G  Z  T  U  Q  O
L  I  H  T  P  J  U  T  Y  Q  U  S
F  M  N  F  L  E  U  R  O  P  A  S
T  M  B  A  Z  O  R  S  M  V  R  E
Y  A  R  D  C  U  F  J  N  I  T  S
A  G  C  S  H  O  Q  F  A  K  R  S
I  E  S  T  R  I  N  G  E  I  R  I
F  O  U  R  T  H  D  O  W  N  J  O
S  T  I  F  F  A  R  M  K  G  S  N
E  H  A  S  H  M  A  R  K  S  B  E
R  E  S  T  R  A  I  N  I  N  G  V
```

100

SOLUTION 5

```
L E G W H I P L W A O P
Z X I B F R A U X E B H
D D F U I R S P N A U I
G U L T E Y S B C T B L
Z C E T L I A A P X B A
O M A O D B T C K J L D
A L F N G U T K B U E E
P E L H O X E M O M S L
Q I I O A T M X O B C P
H G C O L Y P Z T O R H
M W K K P T T A L F E I
Y K E L Z U P V E J E A
Q J R L S H O T G U N Z
Z B L A C K M O N D A Y
```

SOLUTION 6

```
M G B I T J L K G N C O
R E A L P A S R P O H D
I N C L Q C N P W S A Z
B D K E U K E I X E M F
P A F G I O A T R T P A
F R I A C M K T A I O L
V O E L K A O S I C N S
U U L M K H C B D K S E
T N D O I K A U E L H S
D D E I H O R R S I I T
M O E K H O G S I P A R
T G W O Y Y P H K T P R
C O R N E R B A C K D T
Q U A R T E R B A C K C
```

SOLUTION 7

```
P  J  N  G  J  P  B  O  X  G  T  F
S  M  N  F  K  H  Z  S  X  E  R  X
K  I  E  P  W  U  R  U  S  H  K  Y
R  A  W  I  I  Y  C  O  X  C  Z  E
G  M  Y  S  D  H  R  S  A  H  F  L
T  I  O  T  E  P  E  B  T  E  I  L
N  D  R  O  R  F  T  A  O  C  E  O
B  O  K  L  E  A  U  L  U  K  L  W
K  L  G  S  C  T  R  T  C  D  D  F
C  P  I  S  E  T  N  I  H  O  J  L
C  H  A  T  I  E  H  M  D  W  U  A
Z  I  N  R  V  M  P  O  O  N  D  G
A  N  T  I  E  P  Q  R  W  S  G  K
K  S  S  P  R  T  T  E  N  P  E  V
```

SOLUTION 8

```
F  R  E  E  P  L  A  Y  T  I  F  J
O  U  Y  B  F  W  S  B  O  F  U  A
T  I  A  Q  N  C  I  A  U  R  D  C
T  A  R  G  E  T  N  L  C  M  E  K
G  R  D  Y  W  B  G  L  H  E  F  S
A  X  A  J  Y  Z  L  C  B  F  E  O
P  K  G  P  O  V  E  O  A  L  E  N
Z  O  E  D  R  F  W  N  N  A  S  V
A  N  C  I  K  G  I  T  K  N  I  I
B  N  G  K  J  G  N  R  R  K  V  L
G  U  N  N  E  R  G  O  U  E  E  L
X  O  V  G  T  T  W  L  A  F  E  E
W  M  O  N  S  T  E  R  M  A  N  I
E  B  T  U  R  N  O  V  E  R  D  Q
```

102

SOLUTION 9

```
B  R  F  Z  T  F  D  C  F  X  D  A
O  U  I  L  Y  I  L  W  Y  R  S  G
O  N  F  A  E  L  W  A  C  E  W  F
E  N  B  F  F  X  L  M  T  C  R  Q
P  R  S  N  A  P  B  Z  M  E  U  K
B  O  K  I  K  L  J  O  T  I  S  S
S  V  I  C  D  C  O  N  N  V  P  L
I  E  I  I  O  E  U  B  N  E  I  O
E  R  M  A  H  P  K  B  I  R  R  W
T  B  P  I  G  S  K  I  N  L  A  M
W  P  L  A  Y  C  L  O  C  K  L  E
B  Q  K  K  L  Z  G  Q  M  K  X  S
G  N  M  I  N  N  E  S  O  T  A  H
N  F  O  R  W  A  R  D  P  A  S  S
```

SOLUTION 10

```
M  X  W  C  L  E  V  E  L  A  N  D
O  S  E  C  O  N  D  A  R  Y  F  V
P  A  S  S  B  D  E  G  E  K  A  S
Z  E  A  F  H  P  A  O  C  W  I  U
N  X  N  F  C  H  D  A  B  A  R  C
J  T  F  W  O  A  B  L  T  S  C  E
X  R  R  A  V  L  A  L  W  H  A  S
T  A  A  L  E  F  L  I  C  I  T  S
I  P  N  K  R  B  L  N  H  N  C  F
D  O  C  O  Y  A  R  E  I  G  H  U
D  I  I  N  F  C  C  R  E  T  K  L
N  N  S  A  H  K  P  O  F  O  I  L
C  T  C  G  O  S  R  Q  S  N  C  L
W  N  O  N  J  S  M  G  H  W  K  Y
```

103

SOLUTION 11

```
P O S T P A T T E R N  N    L
I N C O M P L E T E  C     O
D  S  T U N T  F X X V K    N
C H A R G E R S  V W Q     G
K I G U I  J A G U A R S    S
O F J N C P L O P Z A      N
U T Y P O X S L S H U      A
L  T E A M M A T E  K  K    P
G R A S P I N G  R L  I     P
O P S S L W C L Q C  C     E
Y Q S J E G E K V I  K     R
M B V  A T L A N T A  L     S
Y J X D E C D Q W L L      G
N E W O R L E A N S  J W
```

SOLUTION 12

```
I N D I R E C T S N A P
G M C P I B S A M J S N
W A I M L E D A V G N D
X N T K L G S P I K E Y
M O A B E Z P K T F W J
Z E M Y G F E I K B E Z
U U P E A J C C B I N O
F V A A L U I K A J N N
G R B L S K A S G M L E
W E A O H E L I I S A B
L I Y C I B J X E K N L
I W O Y F O R W A R D I
V O E S T D B T Q C N T
P L A C E K I C K Z P Z
```

104

SOLUTION 13

```
E  V  E  Y  J  F  G  A  C  C  W  D
I  M  A  M  I  I  R  B  O  U  A  A
T  A  C  K  L  E  E  A  F  T  O  L
A  U  D  I  B  L  E  F  B  B  Y  L
M  S  C  J  N  D  N  L  I  L  D  A
S  C  R  Z  L  P  B  C  N  O  O  S
F  R  O  J  T  O  B  A  C  C  U  C
A  A  S  U  D  S  Y  R  O  K  B  O
P  M  S  P  N  I  Q  R  R  I  L  W
I  B  B  M  V  T  V  I  N  N  E  B
U  L  A  A  I  I  E  E  E  G  W  O
R  E  R  N  G  O  C  R  R  F  I  Y
C  I  N  C  I  N  N  A  T  I  N  S
S  C  V  W  I  L  D  C  A  T  G  L
```

SOLUTION 14

```
Y  S  X  F  M  O  V  E  K  L  F  S
S  M  Z  M  K  K  D  H  L  M  W  F
C  A  R  O  L  I  N  A  Y  A  F  U
P  S  K  L  S  U  B  L  G  N  N  M
L  H  B  F  T  E  O  O  A  I  F  B
H  M  F  S  V  C  P  V  T  F  O  L
H  O  F  I  M  E  P  I  E  N  R  E
W  U  L  G  B  N  O  L  D  I  M  R
T  T  D  D  J  T  N  A  R  M  A  O
D  H  J  D  E  E  E  T  I  O  T  O
P  N  R  E  L  R  N  I  O  T  I  S
G  V  I  J  A  E  T  V  N  I  O  K
R  Z  N  F  A  L  C  O  N  S  N  I
J  P  S  C  O  R  I  N  G  W  Z  J
```

SOLUTION 15

```
X  F  G  F  I  N  B  O  U  N  D  S
D  B  M  P  X  H  P  C  H  P  O  F
L  B  H  A  T  Y  O  O  E  U  U  A
P  I  E  C  F  I  O  C  A  L  B  C
M  K  N  K  A  I  O  R  D  L  L  E
K  N  E  E  L  Q  R  V  C  I  E  M
I  F  O  R  M  A  T  I  O  N  R  A
D  B  B  S  R  A  G  U  A  G  E  S
G  K  C  H  A  I  N  B  C  Z  V  K
F  A  I  R  C  A  T  C  H  M  E  L
B  Q  C  O  M  M  A  N  D  E  R  S
B  A  C  K  W  A  R  D  P  A  S  S
O  X  L  I  N  E  B  A  C  K  E  R
V  R  U  N  N  I  N  G  B  A  C  K
```

SOLUTION 16

```
A  S  P  P  U  M  P  F  A  K  E  E
J  T  F  D  R  A  W  P  L  A  Y  Q
R  E  S  P  L  I  T  E  N  D  G  M
M  E  L  R  E  D  Z  O  N  E  A  I
E  L  A  D  M  G  Z  B  C  E  B  Y
I  E  N  F  Z  I  A  W  T  X  U  P
G  R  T  S  R  P  F  L  V  J  S  L
H  S  K  A  N  S  A  S  C  I  T  Y
O  V  E  R  T  I  M  E  F  D  E  O
G  A  I  R  C  O  R  Y  E  L  L  S
S  U  P  E  R  B  O  W  L  G  P  Z
Z  L  P  Q  L  A  S  V  E  G  A  S
U  S  T  A  R  T  E  R  C  T  P  S
L  O  T  E  N  N  E  S  S  E  E  W
```

106

SOLUTION 17

```
P  Z  B  L  I  T  Z  A  T  Z  D  H
N  R  I  U  E  A  I  P  I  H  E  O
E  E  T  W  B  I  Q  F  G  A  F  U
Z  C  A  R  G  L  H  K  H  N  E  S
S  E  J  G  F  B  C  T  T  D  N  T
C  I  I  O  E  A  G  L  E  S  S  O
X  V  Z  K  S  C  R  K  N  T  I  N
S  E  G  Y  J  K  I  I  D  E  V  T
S  R  T  T  P  R  D  C  U  A  E  E
K  U  W  E  A  K  I  K  I  M  B  X
H  G  O  A  L  A  R  E  A  R  A  A
G  U  Q  H  S  Y  O  R  C  J  C  N
C  L  I  P  P  I  N  G  R  B  K  S
I  N  D  I  A  N  A  P  O  L  I  S
```

SOLUTION 18

```
B  L  O  C  K  I  N  G  S  L  E  D
D  R  I  V  E  N  Y  T  W  Y  I  P
F  N  B  L  J  V  A  K  I  I  H  X
B  Z  D  I  R  E  C  T  S  N  A  P
L  P  B  A  D  A  Y  F  H  J  R  E
F  A  R  H  B  A  C  K  B  U  D  X
R  T  L  E  S  O  I  S  O  R  C  T
N  R  M  T  C  Y  H  A  E  E  O  R
U  I  L  C  V  E  F  I  D  U  A
D  O  K  M  M  H  P  N  Y  W  N  T
C  T  W  S  P  L  I  T  T  H  T  I
C  S  Y  N  Z  B  R  S  I  Y  J  M
A  G  N  V  I  L  R  V  I  O  J  E
R  E  V  E  R  S  E  Z  B  H  N  G
```

107

SOLUTION 19

```
S  T  D  O  A  N  S  X  E  T  Q  F
C  O  N  T  A  I  N  P  O  I  M  A
E  N  D  Z  O  N  E  H  L  C  R  N
H  D  E  F  E  N  S  E  X  A  F  T
N  F  J  C  X  P  K  U  W  R  Y  A
P  A  S  S  I  N  G  Y  A  R  D  S
X  C  C  H  A  B  F  E  I  Y  B  Y
F  H  C  B  N  B  X  B  V  F  U  J
S  J  Y  Q  B  M  S  R  E  B  J  X
U  L  Q  L  Z  L  W  Y  D  O  H  X
T  R  U  E  F  R  E  S  H  M  A  N
P  A  C  K  A  G  E  W  B  B  M  Z
M  M  T  Y  I  H  P  Z  P  J  V  L
D  S  E  A  H  A  W  K  S  M  Z  Y
```

SOLUTION 20

```
F  R  E  E  S  A  F  E  T  Y  W  V
N  S  S  U  A  B  S  N  R  D  F  P
I  U  V  L  P  A  N  T  H  E  R  S
H  U  M  A  N  T  O  M  A  N  N  D
H  O  L  D  I  N  G  K  L  V  Q  V
D  X  J  P  A  N  C  A  K  E  B  O
A  S  K  V  I  I  V  X  S  R  B  P
K  G  N  C  K  W  O  H  H  B  E  P
C  U  I  E  R  B  D  S  O  R  N  O
J  A  E  R  N  A  I  A  O  O  G  S
B  R  O  W  N  S  V  F  T  N  A  I
F  D  O  P  G  K  L  E  I  C  L  N
X  D  V  C  S  F  O  T  N  O  S  G
E  S  E  Y  F  A  J  Y  G  S  V  I
```

Made in the USA
Monee, IL
18 November 2023